EAT LOTS OF COLORS

A Colorful Look at Healthy Nutrition for Children

Revised Edition

Written by Helen Marstiller

Masters of Science in Holistic Nutrition

www.eatlotsofcolors.com

eatlotsofcolors@gmail.com

Illustrated by Valerie Bouthyette
www.vbouthyette.com

Eat Lots of Colors
A Colorful Look at Healthy Nutrition for Children
Revised Edition

© 2013 Helen Marstiller
Masters of Science in Holistic Nutrition

P.O. Box 353
Washington DC 20044

Available on Amazon.com

Printed in the United States of America

It is with adoration and admiration
that I dedicate this book to my sister, Merrie,
who devoted herself to
the nurturing, development and well- being of children.

There's a reason for this book.
It matters a lot.

There are two kinds of foods.
Some are good.
Some are not.
Learn to give food you eat thought.

Good foods grow on vines.
They come from bushes.
Find them on trees.
They grow whole from the ground.
They come in all colors.
In nature they're found.

From colors whole foods get their magic.
Ignore this?
It would be tragic!

Here's the deal.
Some foods aren't real....

They've been treated.
They're packaged.
Their colors are fake.
It's not good to eat these.
Not every day!

Eat whole foods in colors.
They have power to heal.
Tell your mother! And your brother!
See how good you can feel!

Red

Boost your brain.
Eat juicy red berries.
Make learning easy.
Eat apples and cherries!

Red veggies taste really great.
Go on. Have some.
Celebrate!

Get off of your seat!
Get onto your feet!

Your body's a gift.
Learn how to eat well.
Move it.
Get fit!

Red

Cherries
Cranberries
Pomegranate
Raspberries
Red Apple
Red Grapefruit
Red Grapes
Red Pepper
Red Potato
Rhubarb
Strawberries
Tomato
Watermelon

Orange

Carrots give your eyes sparkle.
It's a fact.
It's remarkable!

Oranges taste better than candy.
Dried peaches come in handy.

Mango is sweet.
Cantaloupe? Make it a treat!

Put mangos into your cart.
Don't forget nectarines!
They're good for your heart.

Orange

Apricot
Butternut Squash
Cantaloupe
Clementine
Mango
Nectarine
Orange
Orange Pepper
Papaya
Peach
Pumpkin
Sweet Potato
Yam

Yellow

Pineapple is sassy.
Grapefruit is classy.

Lemon is tart.
Pears make you smart.

Want to play cello?
Forget the marshmallows!
Eat real foods that are yellow.

Yellow

Banana
Lemon
Pineapple
Summer Squash
Yellow Apple
Yellow Corn
Yellow Grapefruit
Yellow Onion
Yellow Pear
Yellow Pepper
Yellow Wax Beans

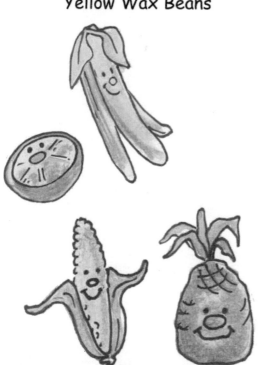

Green

Want to feel strong?
Belt out a song?

Eat something green.
You'll never go wrong.

Some apples and beans are green.
Greens help you stay lean.

Put lime into your water.
It'll be more nutritious.
It'll taste tarter.

Eat broccoli and peas.
Try lettuce and sprouts.
Greens clean your tummy.
Give greens a shout!

Green

Artichoke
Asparagus
Avocado
Broccoli
Broccolini
Brussels Sprouts
Celery
Collard Greens
Cucumber
Edamame
Green Apple
Green Beans
Green Cabbage
Green Grapes
Green Olives
Green Pear
Green Pepper
Honeydew Melon
Kale
Kiwi
Lettuce
Lime
Peas
Spinach
Winter Squash

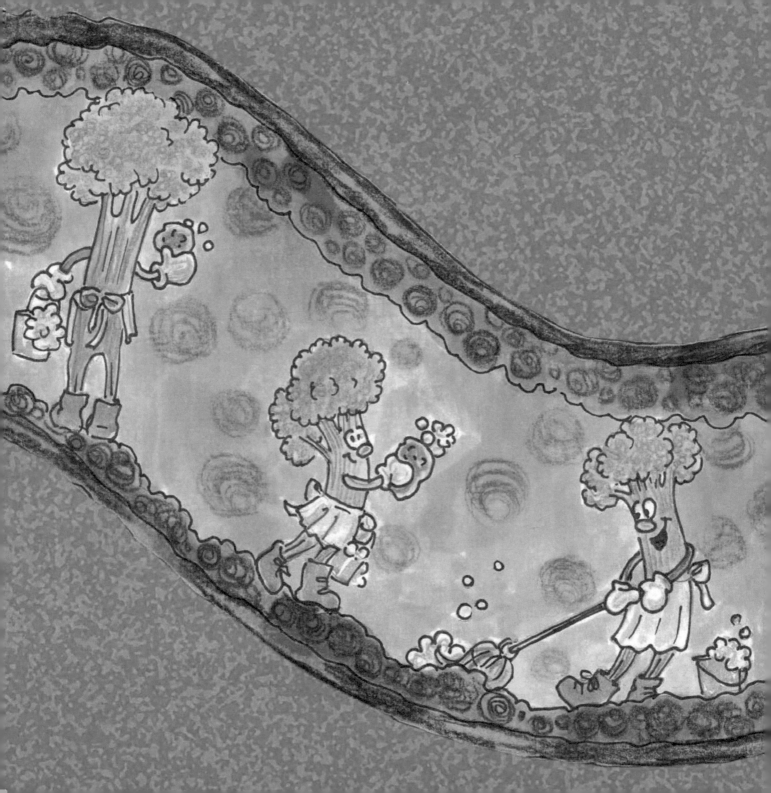

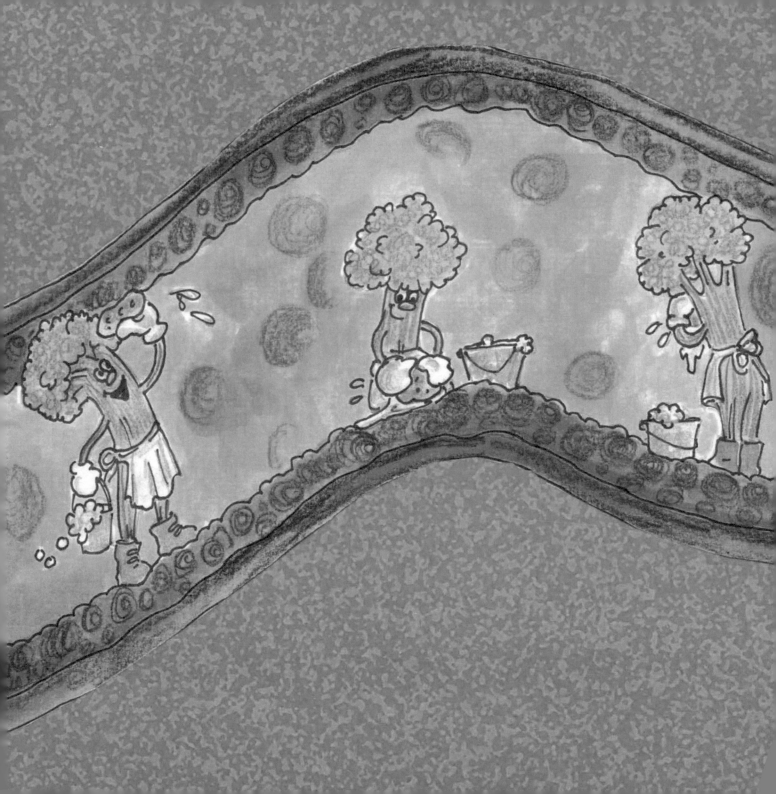

Brown

Brown pears are crunchy.
Dip them in peanut butter.
Try them with honey.

Brown nuts are yummy to taste.
They're good for your heart.
They're good for a race.

Have something brown!
Don't put it off.
Don't wait!

Skip, jump and laugh. Even twirl!
Try eating brown.
Give it a whirl!

Brown

Barley
Brown Pear
Brown Rice
Dates
Figs
Mushrooms
Nuts
Pumpernickel
Rye
Whole Grain
Whole Wheat

Blue

There aren't many blue foods.
Keep your eyes open.
You will find them.
Wow! They are potent!

Blueberries may keep you healthy.
Go ahead; it's OK.
Have several helpings.

Then go play in the sun.
Have fun!
Hula, skip, swing and run!

Eat something blue.
Make sure you chew. Cows do.
Chewing is good for you too!

Blue

Blueberries
Blue Corn
Blue Potato
Blue Cauliflower
Blue Seaweed

White

Fly a kite?
Better eat white!

Ride a bike?
Boost with white!

Pants getting tight?
Have something white!
Try popcorn.
It beats chips for your hips.

Onions and garlic add flavor.
They're delicious.
So savor!

White

Cauliflower
Coconut
Garlic
Jicama
Oatmeal
Onion
Leek
Parsnip
Popcorn
Pumpkin Seeds
Quinoa
Rice
Turnip
White Beans
White Corn
White Eggplant
White Potato

Black

Snack attack?
Try something black!

Try nori. It's seaweed.
Snack on black seeds.

Black beans have protein.
Trade them for meat.
Wrap beans in tortillas.
What an after-school treat!

Black is like white.
It's not really a color.
That's a fact!
Black will keep you on track.

Black

Blackberries
Black Beans
Black Olives
Black Rice
Nori (Sushi Wrappers)
Poppy Seeds
Prunes
Raisins
Sunflower Seeds

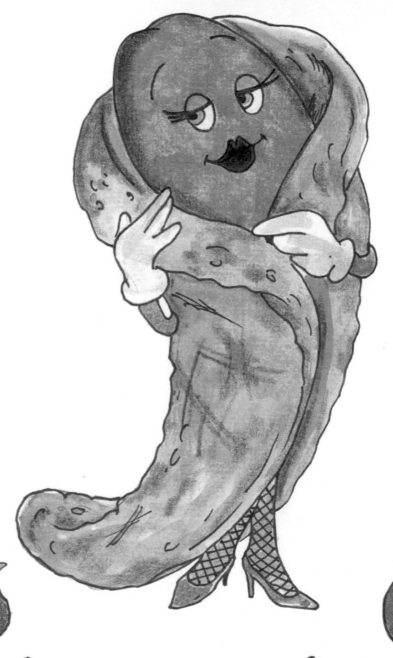

Purple

Slow as a turtle?
Eat foods that are purple.
You'll fly past those hurdles!

Purple cool pop?
All that sugar and dye!
No way!
Stay away!
Don't be misled.
Grab a few grapes instead.

Real foods rule!
So be cool.
Eat your colors.
Keep them real.
See how good you will feel!

Purple

Beet
Cabbage
Eggplant
Grapes
Plum
Purple Onion

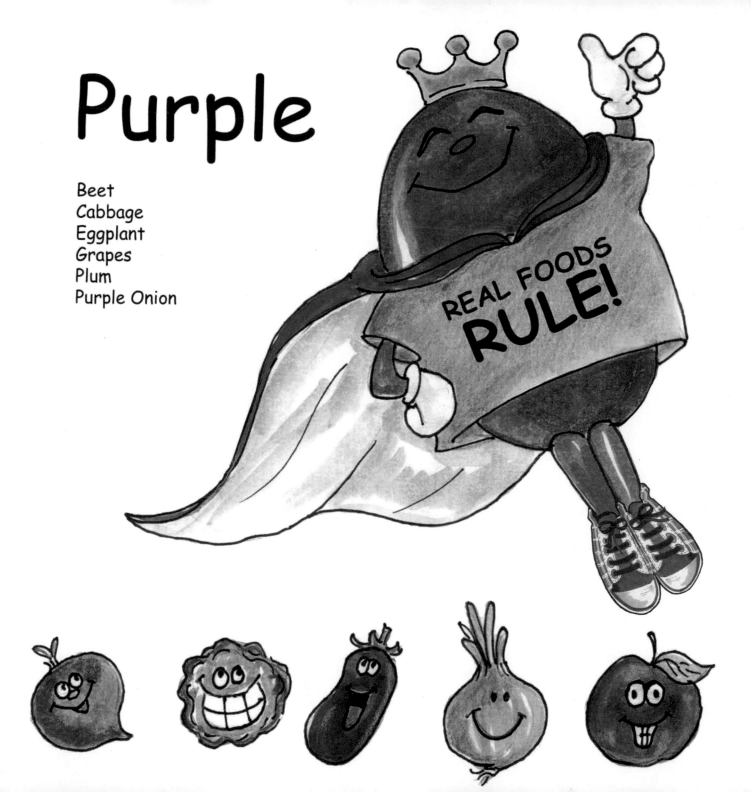

Use this chart to check off each good colored food that you eat every day.
Try to eat one real colored food at each meal. And, be sure to include colorful snacks.
The more colors you can check in a day, the better!
You might want to make copies of this chart each week to
put on your refrigerator, and use colored crayons or pencils for your check marks.

	Red	Orange	Yellow	Green	Brown	Blue	White	Black	Purple
Sunday									
Monday									
Tuesday									
Wednesday									
Thursday									
Friday									
Saturday									

Use this chart to check off each good colored food that you eat every day.
Try to eat one real colored food at each meal. And, be sure to include colorful snacks.
The more colors you can check in a day, the better!
You might want to make copies of this chart each week to
put on your refrigerator, and use colored crayons or pencils for your check marks.

	Red	Orange	Yellow	Green	Brown	Blue	White	Black	Purple
Sunday									
Monday									
Tuesday									
Wednesday									
Thursday									
Friday									
Saturday									

Use this chart to check off each good colored food that you eat every day.
Try to eat one real colored food at each meal. And, be sure to include colorful snacks.
The more colors you can check in a day, the better!
You might want to make copies of this chart each week to
put on your refrigerator, and use colored crayons or pencils for your check marks.

	Red	Orange	Yellow	Green	Brown	Blue	White	Black	Purple
Sunday									
Monday									
Tuesday									
Wednesday									
Thursday									
Friday									
Saturday									

Use this chart to check off each good colored food that you eat every day.
Try to eat one real colored food at each meal. And, be sure to include colorful snacks.
The more colors you can check in a day, the better!
You might want to make copies of this chart each week to
put on your refrigerator, and use colored crayons or pencils for your check marks.

	Red	Orange	Yellow	Green	Brown	Blue	White	Black	Purple
Sunday									
Monday									
Tuesday									
Wednesday									
Thursday									
Friday									
Saturday									

44135327R00020